HOLD ME UP

Noble Drew Ali's Lessons on Law & Spirituality

Prepared by
Bro. Kudjo Adwo El
Grand Sheik, Divine Minister
Moorish Science Temple of America
Subordinate Temple #5-Canaanland

Edited by
Sis. Tauheedah S.
Najee-Ullah El
Managing Editor
Califa Media Publishing

© 2021 Califa Media Publishing

Hold Me Up
Noble Drew Ali Lessons on Law & Spirituality

© 2021
Califa Media Publishing
Lafayette, Indiana

Prepared by
Bro. Kudjo Adwo El
Grand Sheik, Divine Minister
Moorish Science Temple of America
Subordinate Temple #5 — Canaanland

Edited by
Sis. Tauheedah S. Najee-Ullah El
Managing Editor
Califa Media Publishing
CalifaMedia.com

ISBN-13: 978-1-952828-12-6
Library of Congress Control Number: 2021946027

All Rights Reserved. Without Prejudice. No Part Of This Book May Be Reproduced Or Transmitted In Any Form By Any Means, Electronic, Photocopying, Mechanical, Recording, Information Storage Or Retrieval System Unless For The Liberation Of Minds And Gaining Knowledge Of Self.

Cover Design by Sis. T. Najee-Ullah El
Califa Media Publishing

Contents

Moorish American Prayer i

Introduction ii

Noble Drew Ali and Spirituality 1

Noble Drew Ali and Law 34

Other Titles By Kudjo El 72

Moorish American Prayer

•••••

Allah

Father of the Universe, the Father
of Love, Truth, Peace, Freedom and Justice. ALLAH
is my Protection, my Guide and my Salvation By Night
and by Day, through Her Holy Prophet Noble Drew Ali.

•••••

AMEN

Introduction

The master is master only because he is linked to a higher authority, at whose command he acts and to which he is responsible. When he mediates between heaven and earth, he always acts at its bidding. He never claims to be the source himself, , but refers to a higher reality, to an otherworldly authority, to God or to his own master. His submission to this authority and veneration for those who have served it before him are an intrinsic part of what he is and does. It's presence shapes and infuses all his "ceremonial" actions.

The Call for the Master
Karlfried Graf von Dürckheim
From "The Inner Journey: Views from the Buddhist Tradition"
Parabola Anthology Series 2005

Seventh book authored...

Seven years after the release of his first title...

Thirteen years after coming into Moorish Science...

Result: A timely digest for the enlightenment and edification of the Moorish community.

Initially, I thought this to be a book on holding up the Prophet Drew Ali, but as I read, there was another message as well: to save the nations, hold up the woman. By uplifting the Moorish Moslem woman, we uplift all of humanity as the degradation of her mental and spiritual state is directly reflected in the current state of all nations today. After reading the Grand Sheik's latest exploration of the Moorish movement, I came away with an elevated sense of pride, mission, and obligation. To be worthy of such lofty consideration — that your well-being is directly tied to that of the entire world — impels one to prove themselves worthy of such.

This analysis is inspiring and uplifting, outlining the tools left to us by our Prophet, and breaking down their use. Employing an informal yet insistent tone when discussing the importance of recognition of the teachings of Prophet Drew Ali, and the importance of matriarch by the nations and by her self, Grand Sheik Kudjo Adwo El demonstrates why he proves himself worthy of the title Master.

Your Sister in Islam,
Sis. Tauheedah Naje-Ullah El
Managing Editor
Califa Media Publishing

Noble Drew Ali and Spirituality

When we take time to analyze the lessons of Noble Drew Ali, it brings to attention the fact that he was a prophet and his prophesies have been manifesting since his assassination in 1929. Like the Prophets of Old, Noble Drew Ali did the work necessary to get The People to recognize their worth; that the people who apply the lessons will be doing even greater works than they the Prophets came to do. However, that work doesn't make everyone a prophet.

prophet (n.)

late 12c., *"person who speaks for God; one who foretells, inspired preacher,"* from Old French *prophete, profete* "prophet, soothsayer" (11c., Modern French *prophète*) and directly from Latin *propheta*, from Greek *prophētēs* (Doric *prophatēs*) *"an interpreter, spokesman, proclaimer; a harbinger"* (as cicadas of summer), but especially *"one who speaks for a god, inspired preacher or teacher,"* from *pro* "before" (from PIE root *per- (1) "forward," hence "in front of, before") + root of *phanai* "to speak" (from PIE root *bha- (2) "to speak, tell, say").

Noble Drew Ali spoke in a language simple enough for a child to innerstand, so it is incomprehensible that adults do not get this. However, see as brown-skinned people call themselves "black," it becomes obvious why they won't receive the Prophet's message. The Circle 7 is the Master Seal of the Earth plane. The Circle also symbolizes the womb, with man being the 7 within that womb. The Circle is the planet Earth, which is a mother. The four gaps represent the four directions; the seven within the four quadrants stands for perfected man. Standing on the Earth plane, going east, west, north and south or to the hedges and the highways, spreading the Logos or the Word known as Uplifting Fallen Humanity. The four gaps let you know that it is the Master's Seal, and if you have it, you're supposed to be a master. The Master's Seal are four high priests:

Earth, Air, Fire and Water. These are astrological, not religious.

No one aside from Noble DrewAli informed us of our being Moorish scientists. This is not religion. Though it says holy, the Circle 7 Holy Koran is not a holy book; it is a metaphysical book just like all holy books. Only those who adhere to the universal laws, nature's law, common law and Constitutional law can use The Koran in its full capacity — everyone else thinks that it to be some religious book. Don't let views and subscriber-counts fool you out of your birthright. Hearts and likes are not what the Moorish paradigm is about. The Moorish paradigm is not about getting out of tickets or claiming houses. The Moorish paradigm is not about beating some case in court. The Moorish paradigm is about that Circle and that 7 being man's attaining deific life, or man raising his chakras so that he lives on the seventh chakra. That is where every one is supposed to be if they are on the Earth plane. If you made it to this plane in human form, you should be resonating, vibrating on the seventh chakra and higher. Anywhere other than the seventh or higher, you still have serious work to do on this plane. The quadrants are four: 90 degrees, 90 degrees, 90 degrees, 90 degrees. When added, these equal 360 degrees which is knowledge. Ninety degrees and 90 degrees, 90 degrees, 90 degrees are 360 degrees, which is completion. Three-hundred-sixty is also nine because nine is completion and three + six + zero = nine. Additionally when examining four 90 degree quadrants: nine + zero = nine; nine + nine + nine + nine = 36, which is also nine (3+6).

Other than Noble Drew Ali on the cover of the 101 Koran questions, Dr. York El with the mummy in front the pyramid, and the legend of Popocatepetl and Iztaccihuatl, no one was shown holding the mother because this high science brought by Noble Drew Ali is ANCIENT and really all about uplifting wombmen.

Cover for the 101 Koran Questions for Moorish Americans

Malachi Z. York rendition of the cover Prophet Drew Ali's 101 Questionnaire

Leyenda de los Volcanes Animada: The Legend of Popocatepetl & Iztaccíhuatl

If people could use their common sense they would see the message being conveyed: Noble Drew Ali is holding a mother; holding onto grandma; holding Woman in his arms while he's coming out of the Cares of the World, standing on the solid rock of Salvation. Why is he bringing woman out of the water? As one can see, the woman has written on her "Humanity." That was purposefully done. So, the people who think Drew Ali is a patriarch need to recognize that he was the director of the matriarchy. The sister / mother / aunt / grandma is unconscious; she's not awake. She's not dead because she is Humanity and you cannot kill Humanity. Because there will always to be a woman, Humanity can't die.

The Prophet is holding a woman in his arms. On her is written "Humanity." He is not holding a brother *and* a sister with "Humanity" written on *them*. Why would he bring woman out of the cares of the world? Why wouldn't he be holding a brother? If he's a patriarch, he should be holding a brother, no? Clearly, he's not a patriarch. Clearly, he's a matriarch. Clearly, he was the resurrector of the matriarchal mindset; of having honours for mother.

Put your penis away and focus on the vagina. Stop the homosexual patriarchal b.s. If you're pushing patriarchal, you're pushing the homo-erotic European mindset. Matriarch is what rules. Who is the head of the household? Again, according to Noble Drew Ali on the *101 Questionnaire*, if this was about patriarchy and uplifting man, our mission would be the Uplifting Fallen Patriarchy. We are not instructed to uplift fallen patriarchy; we are called to Uplift Fallen Humanity. Why? Because Humanity is woman. It's written right there on the *Koran Questionnaire* — why is it so hard for some to realize what's going on? Are you just dumb or are you stupid or are you incompetent, dumb and stupid? Few teachers before the Prophet Drew Ali spoke of bringing the matriarch back. He was not here for some patriarchal Roman pseudo-concepts. He was here to lift a woman back to her position because, once you raise woman, humanity that comes from her womb will be in the right place automatically.

Masculine cannot do this as there is no masculine being on this planet able to give birth to humanity. Only woman can do that—only woman.

We know that many of these individuals hating on the matriarchy come from a single parent household, so they weren't afforded a full perspective. In these times, most people's mom are their dad as well. The majority of people who come from broken homes end up staying with their Mom Dukes. When there's a divorce, the children usually want to go with Mom — when they need their ass beat or are too much for Mom, they are shipped off to Pops (remember *Boyz n the Hood* and *Concrete Cowboys*).

Why do you think that is? Why do you think that Society is set up where, in most cases, if there is child support, the dad has to pay and (in most cases) not the mom? Why do you think that is? Because women don't run anything? Women run everything. Even in their unconscious state, they run everything because everything has to go through a woman, because everything's feminine. That's just what it is, not to be mad about it. Don't be mad; get in line and recognize what has to be done: we must uplift fallen humanity if we're going to get right.

I come from a two parent household; I had both my mom and my dad in the house, so I don't come from a broken home. When I was growing up, my mom ran the show. If we're going to go somewhere, Mom is the one who's taking Dad's check and saving the money for the trip. If a trip's getting booked, Mom's booking it. If food's getting cooked, Mom's cooking it. Only thing dad did was discipline. And only thing he did other than discipline is what Mom told him to do. That's just what it is: he had his own free time to do whatever he wanted when his time allowed, like go with the boys and all that. But when he came home late, or supposed to be home early and gets in trouble, who's going to the couch? Not mother. No matter how old the man is, he will always be a son to mother. That's just what it is. I'm telling you this because I come from a two parent household WHERE MOM RULED.

Let's look at the example of a baby in a single parent household. If the child is abandoned by one of the parents, you'd better hope it's not the mom. Babies need their mother for the first seven years of their life, especially the early years because of the connection to mother formed during the nine months of gestation. Imagine: being so connected to mother, then taken out of mother and put in the hands of a man you don't know. You don't know him because he's always been outside of yourself. When you're with mother, you're inside; when you're outside of the womb, you're still connected to inside. This is why midwives advise against cutting the umbilical cord after birth. Wait. Let that process happen naturally; let the umbilical cord dissolve because there is a connection the child has to mother that should not be severed immediately after delivery.

Remember: no matter how old he gets, a man is always a son. No matter how old, no matter how old masculine, he is always a son. He is never father, uncle, granddad and all those titles. He's always a son. Take it from a mama's boy. Always a son and Mom always look to protect. That's why mothers keep the sons around and kick the daughters out the house: they are know she is actually is a woman not a daughter. They'll do whatever to keep the son at home because he's always son. He is always a baby boy. There are grown men right now and their mom calling them my baby — why? He's always the son.

Look at a properly run household and you would see that mother runs it. You never, ever, ever, ever, ever, ever, ever, ever hear of mother having to sleep on the couch because she did something wrong. Never. It's always that father has to go to the doghouse. Never, ever do you hear Mom goes to the doghouse or Mom did something messed up; that she didn't do the dishes or whatever, so she has to sleep on the couch that night because Dad's mad and he wants the bed for himself. Matriarch rules, but matriarch must also know that she can't be a ding bat and expect to rule the Empire. Wombman must return to her ancestral mindset if there is to be a harmonious transition from the dead state to the matriarchal.

Keep in mind sons: Chapters 20, 22 as well as 31, 32, 33, 34 of the Holy Koran of MSTA/MHTS include qualities that are feminine in nature.

CHAPTER XX. Holy Instruction and Warnings for All Young Men

1. Beware, young man, beware of all the allurements of wantonness, and let not the harlot tempt thee to excess in her delights.
2. The madness of desire shall defeat its own pursuits; from the blindness of its rage, thou shalt rush upon destruction.
3. Therefore give not up thy heart to her sweet enticements, neither suffer thy soul to be enslaved by her enchanting delusions
4. The fountain of health which must supply the stream of pleasure, shall quickly be dried up, and every spring of joy shall be exhausted.
5. In the prime of thy life old age shall overtake thee; the sun shall decline in the morning of thy days.
6. But when virtue and modesty enlighten her charms, the luster of a beautiful woman is brighter than the stars of Heaven and the influence of her power it is in vain to resist.
7. The whiteness of her bosom transcendeth the lily; her smile is more delicious than a garden of roses.
8. The innocence of her eyes is like that of the turtle; simplicity and truth dwell in her heart.
9. The kisses of her mouth are sweeter than honey; the perfumes of Arabia breathe from her lips.
10. Shut not thy bosom to the tenderness of love; the purity of its flame shall ennoble thy heart, and soften it to receive the fairest impressions.

203. Bro. O. Payton-Bey of Temple #4 and #25 said that the Holy Prophet Noble Drew Ali said, "**If you have a wife, and she does not belong to the Temple, instead of giving her one apple, give her two.**"

CHAPTER XXII. Duty of a Husband

1. Take unto thyself a wife and obey the ordinance of Allah; take unto thyself a wife, and become a faithful member of society.
2. But examine with care, and fix not suddenly. On thy present choice depends thy future happiness.
3. If much of her time is destroyed in dress and adornment; if she is enamored with her own beauty, and delighted with her own praise; if she laugheth much, and talketh loud; if her foot abideth not in her father's house, and her eyes with boldness rove on the faces of men; though her beauty were as the sun in the firmament of heaven, turn thy face from her charms, turn thy feet from her paths, and suffer not thy soul to be ensnared by the allurements of imagination.
4. But when thou findest sensibility of heart, joined with softness of manners; and accomplished mind, with a form agreeable to thy fancy; take her home to thy house; she is worthy to be thy friend, thy companion in life, the wife of thy bosom.
5. O cherish her as a blessing sent to thee from Heaven. Let the kindness of thy behavior endear thee to her heart.
6. She is the mistress of thy house; treat her therefore with respect, that thy servants may obey her.
7. Oppose not her inclination without cause; she is the partner of thy cares, make her also the companion of thy pleasures.
8. Reprove her faults with gentleness, exact not her obedience with rigor.
9. Trust thy secrets in her breast; her counsels are sincere, thou shalt not

be deceived.

10. Be faithful to her bed; for she is mother of thy children.

11. When pain and sickness assault her, let thy tenderness soothe her affliction; a look from thee of pity and love shall alleviate her grief, or instigate her pain and be of more avail than ten physicians.

12. Consider the tenderness of her sex, the delicacy of her frame; and be not severe to her weakness but remember thine own imperfections.

Metaphysical meaning of justice

justice--When judgment is divorced from love, and works from the head alone, there goes forth the human cry for justice. In his mere human judgment man is hard and heartless; he deals out punishment without consideration of motive or cause, and justice goes awry. When justice and love meet at the heart center, there are balance, poise, and righteousness. There is an infinite law of justice that may be called into activity. When we call our inner forces into action, the universal law begins its great work in us, and all the laws both great and small fall into line and work for us. The true way to establish justice is by appealing directly to the divine law. Source: Truthunity.net/rw/justice.

CHAPTER XXXI. Holy Instructions From the Prophet Justice

1. The peace of society dependeth on justice; the happiness of individuals, on the safe enjoyment of all their possessions.

2. Keep the desires of thy heart, therefore, within the bounds of moderation; let the hand of justice lead them aright.

3. Cast not an evil eye on the goods of thy neighbor; let whatever is his property be sacred from thy touch.

4. Let no temptation allure thee, nor any provocation excite thee to lift up

thy hand to the hazard of his life.

5. *Defame him not in his character; bear no false witness against him.*

6. *Corrupt not his servant to cheat or forsake him; and the wife of his bosom, O tempt not to sin.*

7. *It will be a grief to his heart, which thou canst not relieve; an injury to his life, which no reparation can atone.*

8. *In thy dealings with men, be impartial and just; and do unto them as thou wouldst they should do unto thee.*

9. *Be faithful to thy trust, and deceive not the man who relieth upon thee; be assured, it is less evil in the sight of Allah to steal than to betray.*

10. *Oppress not the poor, and defraud not of his hire the laboring man.*

11. *When thou selleth for gain, hear the whispering of conscience, and be satisfied with moderation; nor from the ignorance of thy buyer take any advantage.*

12. *Pay the debts which thou oweth: for he who gave thee credit, relieth upon thine honor; and to withhold from him his due, is both mean and unjust.*

13. *Finally, O son of society, examine thy heart, call remembrance to thy aid; and if in any of these things thou hath transgressed, make a speedy reparation, to the utmost of thy power.*

"*Seva* or selfless service is an important key to spiritual growth. First it should actually be called self-full service. We should give from a cup that runeth over. Fill yourself spiritually in whatever means works for you then give the gift of yourself."- Dr. Stephen Wechsler

CHAPTER XXXII. Holy Instructions From the Prophet <u>Charity</u>

1. Happy is the man who hath sown in his breast the seeds of benevolence: the produce thereof shall be charity and love.

2. From the fountain of his heart shall rise rivers of goodness; and the streams shall overflow, for the benefit of mankind.

3. He assisteth the poor in their trouble; he rejoiceth in furthering the prosperity of all men.

4. He censureth not his neighbor; he believeth not the tales of envy and malevolence; neither repeateth he their slanders.

5. He forgiveth the injuries of men, he wipeth them from his remembrance; revenge and malice have no place in his heart.

6. For evil he returneth not evil, he hateth not even his enemies, but requiteth their injustice with a friendly admonition.

7. The griefs and anxieties of men excite his compassion; he endeavoreth to alleviate the weight of their misfortunes, and the pleasure of success rewardeth his labor.

8. He calmeth the fury, he healeth the quarrels of angry men, and preventeth the mischiefs of strife and animosity.

9. He promoteth in his neighborhood peace and good will, and his name is repeated with praise and benedictions.

Metaphysical meaning of gratitude

gratitude--Gratitude and thanksgiving are both necessary in demonstrating prosperity through divine law. Be grateful to God and thankful to the friends whom He uses to supply you.

All metaphysicians have found by experience that being thankful for what they have increases the inflow. Gratitude is a great mind magnet, and when it is expressed from the spiritual standpoint it is powerfully augmented. The saying of grace at the table has its origin in this idea of the power of increase through giving thanks. Source: Truthunity.net/rw/gratitude.

CHAPTER XXXIII. Holy Instructions From the Prophet Gratitude

1. As the branches of a tree return their sap to the root, from whence it arose; as a river poureth its streams to the sea, whence the spring was supplied; so the heart of a grateful man delighteth in returning a benefit received.
2. He acknowledgeth his obligation with cheerfulness, he looketh on his benefactor with love and esteem.
3. And if to return it be not in his power, he nourisheth the memory of it in his breast with kindness; he forgetteth it not all the days of his life.
4. The heart of the grateful man is like the clouds of heaven which drops upon the earth, fruits, herbage and flowers; but the heart of the ungrateful is like a desert of sand which swalloweth with greediness the showers that fall, and burieth them in its bosom, and produceth nothing.
5. Envy not thy benefactor, neither strive to conceal the benefit he hath conferred; for though to oblige is better than to be obliged, though the act of generosity commandeth admiration, yet the humility toucheth the heart, and is amiable on the sight both of Allah and man.
6. But receive not a favor from the hand of the proud; to the selfish and avaricious have no obligation; the vanity of pride shall expose thee to shame; the greediness of avarice shall never be satisfied.

"Sincerity is one of the requisites for realising God. But just by becoming sincere, one cannot realise God. Ordinary people can be sincere. We see in our day-to-day life many honest people on earth. They don't tell lies. They do not deceive anybody. They do not harm anyone. These people have sincerity. This good habit they got from their parents, or they brought it from their past incarnation. But they are not going to be realised tomorrow or in this incarnation unless they begin to aspire. They are nowhere near realisation. In addition to sincerity, one has to have aspiration, one has to have the soul's inner urge. When we have aspiration, then only do we go consciously toward the Supreme." – Illumination Sri Chinmoy

CHAPTER XXXIV. Holy Instructions From the Prophet <u>Sincerity</u>

1. O thou who are enamored with the beauty of Truth, and hast fixed thy heart on the simplicity of her charms, hold fast thy fidelity unto her, and forsake her not; the constancy of thy virtue shall crown thee with honor.
2. The tongue of the sincere is rooted in heart; hypocrisy and deceit have no place in his words.
3. He blusheth at falsehood, and is founded; but in speaking the truth, he hath a steady eye.
4. He supporteth, as a man, the dignity of his character; to the arts of hypocrisy he scorneth to stoop.
5. He is consistent with himself; he is never embarrassed; he hath courage enough for truth; but to lie he is afraid.
6. He is far above the meanness of dissimulation; the words of his mouth are the thoughts of his heart.
7. Yet, with prudence and caution he openeth his lips; he studieth what is right, and speaketh with discretion.
8. He adviseth with friendship; he reproveth with freedom; and whatsoever he promiseth shall surely be performed.
9. But the heart of the hypocrite is hid in his breast; he maketh his words in the semblance of truth, while the business of his life is only to deceive.
10. He laugheth in sorrow, he weepeth in joy; and the words of his mouth have no interpretation.
11. He worketh in the dark as a mole, and fancieth he is safe; but he blundereth into light, and is betrayed and exposed, with dirt on his head.

12. He passeth his days in perpetual constraint; his tongue and heart are forever at variance.
13. He laboreth for the character of a righteous man; and huggeth himself in the thoughts of his cunning.
14. O fool, fool! The pains which thou taketh to hide what thou art, are more than would make thee what thou wouldst seem; and the children of Wisdom shall mock at thy cunning, when in the midst of security, thy disguise is stripped off, and the finger of derision shall point thee to scorn.

The valley spirit never dies;

It is the woman, primal mother.

Her gateway is the root of heaven and earth.

It is like a veil barely seen.

Use it; it will never fail. - Tao Te Ching

CHAPTER XXXVII. Holy Instructions From the Prophet *The Breath of Heaven*

1. Vaunt not thy body; because it was first formed; nor of thy brain, because therein thy soul resideth. Is not the master of the house more honorable than its walls?
2. The ground must be prepared before corn be planted; the potter must build his furnace before he can make his porcelain.
3. As the breath of Heaven sayeth unto the waters of the deep; "This way shall thy billows roll, and no other; Thus high, and no higher shall they raise their fury"; so let thy spirit, O man, actuate and direct thy flesh; so let it repress its wilderness.
4. Thy body is as the globe of the earth; thy bones the pillars that sustain it on its basis.

5. As the ocean giveth rise to springs, whose waters return again into its bosom through the rivers; so runneth thy life from thy outwards, and so runneth it into its place again.

6. Do not both retain their course forever? Behold, the same Allah ordained them.

7. Is not thy nose the channel to perfumes, thy mouth the path to delicacies.

8. Are not thine eyes the sentinels that watch for thee? Yet how often are they unable to distinguish truth from error?

9. Keep thy soul in moderation; teach thy spirit to be attentive to its good; so shall these its ministers be always to thee conveyances of truth.

10. Thine hand, is it not a miracle? Is there in the creation aught like unto it? Wherefore was it given thee, but that thou mightest stretch it out to the assistance of thy brother?

11. Why of all things living are thou alone made capable of blushing? The world shall read thy shame upon thy face; therefore do nothing shameful.

12. Fear and dismay, which robs thy countenance of its ruddy splendor, avoid guilt, and thou shalt know that fear is beneath thee, that dismay is unnamely.

13. Wherefore to thee alone speaks shadows in the vision of the pillow? Reverence them; for know that dreams are from on high.

14. Thou man alone canst speak. Wonder at thy glorious prerogative; and pay to Him who gave it to thee a rational and welcome praise, teaching thy children wisdom, instructing the offspring of thy loins in piety.

---

101 Koran Questions for Moorish Children

61. What is the modern name for those Angels? Asiatics.

Metaphysical meaning of angel

    angel--A messenger of God; the projection into consciousness of a spiritual idea direct from the Fountainhead, Jehovah. "And there appeared unto him an angel of the Lord standing on the right side of the altar" (Luke 1:11). The word of Truth, in which is centered the power of God to overcome all limited beliefs and conditions.

angel, of Jehovah--The quickening thought of God appearing in the form of light or divine intelligence, intuition, and understanding.

angels, ascending and descending--The imaging power of the mind receiving divine ideas and reflecting them into the consciousness.

angels, office of--To guard, to direct, and to redeem the natural forces of the body and mind, which have in them the future of the whole man. Source: Truthunity.net/rw/angel

---

101 Koran Questions for Moorish Children

64. Give five names that are given to the descendants of Adam and Eve? Lucifer, Satan, Devil, Dragon and Beast.

Metaphysical meaning of day-star

day-star (Lat., Lucifer; Gk., phosphorus; Heb. Or)--the principle of light; anything consisting of light; halo; aurora; power of illumination; a star. The text in Isaiah, "O day-star, son of the morning!" signifies man's uplifting of the ruling ego of the sense consciousness (represented here by the king of Babylon), and attributing to the outer-sense man those qualities of light, understanding, and greatness that belong to God only. This is adverse, of course, and it comes under the Satanic phase of thought in the individual; it must be overthrown, cast down and out of consciousness. Metaphysically interpreted, therefore, this text in Isaiah does refer to Satan, to his self-exaltation and downfall. Source: https://www.truthunity.net/mbd/day-star

Metaphysical meaning of Satan

Satan, sa'-tan (Heb.)--lier in wait; an adversary; an enemy; hater; accuser; opposer; contradictor.

The same as the Devil, the Adversary, the Evil One, and the like (Job. 1:6-12; Matt. 4:10).

Meta. The deceiving phase of mind in man that has fixed ideas in opposition to Truth (adversary, lier in wait, accuser, opposer, hater, an enemy). Satan assumes various forms in man's consciousness, among which may be mentioned egotism, a puffing up of the personality; and the opposite of this, self-deprecation, which admits the "accuser" into the consciousness. This "accuser" makes man believe that he is inherently evil.

Satan is the "Devil," a state of mind formed by man's personal ideas of his power and completeness and sufficiency apart from God. Besides at times puffing up the personality, this satanic thought often turns about and, after having tempted one to do evil, discourages the soul by accusing it of sin. Summed up, it is the state of mind in man that believes in its own sufficiency independent of its creative Source: https://www.truthunity.net/mbd/satan

Dragon

Known as Quetzalcoatl, Kukulkan was worshiped as the great 'feathered serpent' god in the pantheon of Aztecs, Toltecs and the Mayans. The major deity (often taking the form of a mythical dragon-like entity) seems to have played a multifaceted role while practicing his 'godly' business. To that end, Kukulkan was the god of creation, the sire of both the Morning and Evening Star, the protector the craftsmen, the rain-maker, the wind-blower and also the fire-bringer. Interestingly, both the Mayans and the Aztecs were not too keen on solar eclipses (given the sacredness of the sun), as such their mythic traditions used to depict such rare scenarios with the Earth Serpent swallowing the great Quetzalcoatl. Furthermore, as opposed to their cultural penchant for human sacrifices, Kukulkan was supposedly not fond of such bloodthirsty practices. Source: https://www..com/2018/03/27/10-mythical-dragon-entities-facts/

Man's Beastly Nature

A person who follows their own mind and urges, has the mind of a beast. Beasts (animals) do things which are natural for them to do. Meat eaters should not be cooking their meat as that's not as a beast does. If you're such a meat eater do like the animals and eat that flesh raw. *A beast cannot recognize a thing of value or beauty because its mind is limited to its beastly capacity.* Most have beauty right in their face and miss it due to the murky ethers of the flesh clouding their spiritual sight. *Beasts are wise according to their natural understanding; they are prisoners of their beastly nature.* Prison is not where man needs to be. If one is imprisoned anywhere, you are not free; if you are not free your purpose will be to serve someone else. *A beast does not realize or comprehend that it is a beast. It does not reason with itself or others. The people who have not realized themselves to be beasts, have not beheld the pure divine physical nature. To believe you are not a beast reveals a mind void of wisdom as every being has within them the beastly nature and it is up to the individual to suppress it and strive for higher thinking.* Most people who claim to be void of beastly nature and lower self vibrations are the most holy and most criminal people on this planet. The ones who claim to have the greatest relationship with God are usually the most beastly. *The realization that man (yourself) is beastly, is Divine understanding. When a person realizes and admits their outward beastly nature, then they have taken a step in the direction* of *Divine self realization. If a person has convinced themselves believing that they have acquired a Divine nature in the flesh, they are fools to do so and ignorantly beastly. Only through the realization of one's beastly nature can there be hope of inspired* redemption *of the higher self.* This is why Noble Drew Ali taught to know your higher AND lower self. In innerstanding the beastly nature of the self one will realize where true enlightenment is. Man is the Lord of all the plane of manifest, of protoplast, of mineral, of plant, of beast, but he gave up his birthrights, just to gratify his lower self. Man will regain his lost estate, his heritage; but he must do it in a conflict that cannot be told in words. Enlightenment is not from words of lips but from actions that man takes to be redeemed mentally and spiritually. So man, the seed, must be deep planted in a soil that he might grow, unfold, as does the bud unfold to show the flower. *Italicized portions from https://branchdavidian.tripod.com/nature.html.*

═══

101 Koran Questions for Moorish Children

65. What is the Devil sometimes called? The lower Self?

Metaphysical meaning of Devil

Devil--The mass of thoughts that has been built up in race consciousness through many generations of earthly experiences and crystallized into what may be termed human personality, or carnal mind, which opposes and rejects God.

The "devil" is a state of consciousness adverse to the divine good. Other names for this state of consciousness are the Adversary, carnal mind, the accuser, and the old man. There is no personal devil. God is the one omnipresent Principle of the universe, and there is no room for any principle of evil, personified or otherwise.

Devil, how to overcome the--The Devil is overcome by denying his existence and by affirming universal Christ love for God and all men. The devils that we encounter are fear, anger, jealousy, and other similar negative traits, and they are in ourselves. Christ gives us the power to cast out these devils, thereby cleansing our consciousness. Source: Metaphysical Bible Dictionary.

---

101 Koran Questions for Moorish Children

70. What is the Higher self? The Higher self is the Mother of the Virtues and the harmonies of life and breeds Justice, Mercy Love and Right.

73. What does the Lower-self breed? Hatred, Slander, Lewdness, Murders, Theft and EVERYTHING that harms.

87. What is meant by the word black? Black according to science means death.

Color Symbolism and Meaning of Black
ColorSensational.com

Black's sober hue is associated with mourning in much of the world. A black mark on your record reveals wrongdoing, and we characterize bed people as being black-hearted. Black is frightening, as it conceals, rather than illuminates, and the cover of night is a perfect scenario for bad behavior. Too much black in design can be overwhelming and dull. In 2014, Burger King introduced black KURO Pearl and KURO Diamond burgers, which came complete with black buns, black cheese, and black sauce in Japan. America's were intrigued so Burger King offered the black burger as a special for Halloween. What in Japan was a hit turned out to not be well received in America, much possibly because in western cultures the color black is seen as a negative, death-like color and unappetizing.

The Esoteric Meaning of colors
BLACK
RuneLore.it

Black absorbs and hides and creates confusion and chaos, new beginnings, knowledge of hidden things, is the container of light, one of the most powerful color. Use black for the self-control, time and patience. Black is also a good color to use to bring discord and confusion within the enemy. It can also be used for protection, wrap negative energy, breaking barriers and blocks, reverse and destroy negative thought forms. It's better if applied to others. Black controls the base chakra, the planet Saturn, the earth element and the original religions, it means new beginning. Satanic alchemy, black represents the step into the void of meditation and transformation.

As an identity, "black" casts people into the lowest form of social and economic status. People classified as "black" are civilly dead in the eyes of the law; not in full life, which is why there is always an expectation from "blacks" of the so-called government to create bills and acts so that they may have rights. These so-called rights are really privileges that can be taken away at any time by the person granting them. John Henrick Clarke said there is nothing wrong with the word black, only that is DOES NOT RELATE TO A COUNTRY. That is a very bold statement and one that should be looked at very seriously by the people who call themselves black.

Hadith and Prophesies of Noble Drew Ali

209. Sister A. Brown El of Temple 4 and 25 said that the Holy Prophet said, **"Some of you Moors are going to throw away your name, just for a morsel of bread."**

"Leaders Say Blacks Want To Be Called 'African-Americans'"
AP News (December 20, 1988)

A group of black leaders, including the Rev. Jesse Jackson, says members of their race would prefer to be called African-Americans rather than blacks.

"Just as we were called colored, but were not that, and then Negro, but not that, to be called black is just as baseless," Jackson said at a news conference Monday after a meeting of the black leaders.

Jackson was joined by former Gary, Ind., Mayor Richard Hatcher, National Urban Coalition President Ramona Edelin, Gloria Toote, a former assistant secretary of the U.S. Department of Housing and Urban Development, and others.

"There are Armenian-Americans and Jewish-Americans and Arab-Americans and Italian-Americans," Jackson said. "And with a degree of accepted and reasonable pride, they connect their heritage to their mother country and where they are now."

The black leaders, meeting to discuss national goals, said they would meet again in Washington on March 3. Many of the leaders at the meeting, including representatives of the National Black Republicans Council, the National Black County Officials and the National Association for the Advancement of Colored People, said the term African-Americans would be a psychological lift.

The Rev. Willie Barrow, president of Operation PUSH, said she will start using the term immediately.

"I'm African-American just like the Polish are Polish-American and Italians are Italian-American," she said. "It's something we've all agreed upon and it's just great."

Cook County Commissioner John Stroger said he already uses the term. "It's appropriate in the light of our origin," he said.

But some said the change was superficial.

"We must have really reached a zenith in the civil rights struggle that we have to now busy ourselves with semantics," said the Rev. B. Herbert Martin, head of Chicago's Human Relations Commission.

However, Martin added, "I think the title or name African-American points us to a higher consciousness in terms of the origin of African people."

"To be called African-Americans has cultural integrity," he said. "It puts us in our proper historical context. Every ethnic group in this country has a reference to some land base, some historical cultural base. African- Americans have hit that level of cultural maturity."

"The secret history of the jazz greats who were freemasons"
The Guardian (2014):

"Start digging into the history of freemasonry and you discover that [Duke] Ellington was just one of many renowned African-American musicians to be inducted into its mysterious world. He was joined by the likes of Nat King Cole, WC Handy, Dizzy Gillespie, Count Basie, Lionel Hampton and Paul Robeson....

"By 1900, Prince Hall masonry had become a forum for politicised African-Americans, with Booker T Washington (1856-1915) and W.E.B. Du Bois (1868-1963) serving as active members. Throughout the 20th century, many key figures in the civil rights movement were attracted to freemasonry. The father of Martin Luther King Jr – Martin Luther King Sr (1900-84) – was a member of the 23rd lodge in Atlanta, Georgia. Medgar Evers, the National Association for the Advancement of Colored People (NAACP) activist who was assassinated in 1963, was a 32nd-degree freemason in Ancient & Accepted Scottish Rite, Southern

Jurisdiction. Thurgood Marshall (1908-93), the first black member of the US Supreme Court, was supported by his Prince Hall lodge in Louisiana. The comedian Richard Pryor (1940-2005) joined a lodge in Peoria, Illinois, while actor and activist Ossie Davis (1917-2005), Paul Robeson (1898-1976) and boxer Sugar Ray Robinson (1921-89) were all active Prince Hall masons. Finally, Shaquille O'neal (2011) and Nelson Mandela (1991) just to name a few."

Many black leaders thought it would be better to claim Prince Hall masonry and other masonic rites than be themselves as taught by their Prophet, Noble Drew Ali. Being themselves means, rather than join a lodge, join the Moorish Science Temple of America and help in the program of uplifting our people and the world. With all these black masons, shouldn't we as a people be uplifted by now? Why does the struggle continue generation after generation with no end in sight?

Hadith and Prophesies of Noble Drew Ali

143. Bro. O. Payton-Bey of Temple 4 and 25 said that the Holy Prophet said, "**I took the cover off all the secret organizations.**"

The secret held by these societies is that they are rooted in Moorish Science and Moorish history. *Moors and Masonry Part 1* by Abdullah El Talib Mosi Bey goes into detail about the Moorish enslavement and ransoming of Europeans from the 1500s through to the 1700s, as well as the colonial Federal Government and the Imperial Divan connection to the heritage of the Moors. In his other book, *The Masonic Compass and Square and Their Connection to Measurement and Timekeeping,* presents masonry in its proper astronomical, geometrical and mind development perspective. These lessons are part of the secrets kept by freemasonry within the confines of its walls, and members take oaths to never to reveal these teachings to outsiders.

In a speech at the Million Man March in 1995, Louis Farrakhan delved into the numerology of a tiny Muslim sect and the secret legends of the masonic order. He also described himself in almost messianic terms, declaring himself a prophet sent by God to show America the evil of its ways, as Jeremiah did for Jerusalem. His speech recounted the masonic legend of Hiram Abiff, a noble king struck down by three ruffians. Farrakhan portrayed African Americans as the king, while the three ruffians were embodied in retired Los Angeles police detective Mark Fuhrman, Sen. Jesse Helms and the late Mississippi segregationist and senator, Theodore G. Bilbo. Not only is Farrakhan tied to masonry, but there is documented evidence that he and other members of the Nation of Islam are connected to M.S.T. of A. #13 in Baltimore, Maryland.

Masons meet with Louis Farrakhan at the home of the Elijah Muhammad. Chicago, 2019.

Let There Be Light by Wishum Gregory

Actor Emanuel Lewis (l.) in Masonic paraphernalia.

**Illustrious John Lewis, 33°
Sovereign Grand Inspector General**

Richard Pryor, Henry Brown Lodge No. 22 in Peoria, IL, Kamar Temple No. 56 Oasis of Springfield Desert of IL.

Dr. Yosef Ben-Jochannan with Masonic brothers.

Hadith and Prophesies of Noble Drew Ali

247. Bro. J. Blakely Bey stated that the Holy Prophet said "**Many of you who think you are running away from the Prophet don't know that the further you run away from me, the closer you are coming to me, and when you wind up running you will be right in my arms.**"

Noble Drew Ali and Law

Hadith and Prophesies of Noble Drew Ali

255. Bro. Edward Mealy El stated that the Holy Prophet told him, "**YOU DO WHAT I TELL YOU, NEVER MIND WHAT THEY SAY, I HAVE GIVEN YOU LAW, KORAN, AND CONSTITUTION, AND I EXPECT YOU TO ENFORCE MY LAW, AND DO WHAT I SAY, NEVER MIND WHAT THEY SAY OR DO. THEY CAN DO NOTHING BUT DIE.**"

256. Bro. Edward Mealy El stated that the Holy Prophet told him, "**Children, there won't be but a few saved; because you are not going to do what I tell you. Your way you want, and your way you are going to have. But your way leads downward Children; So you better do like I tell you. If you do like I tell you, there is a chance for you, if not, there is nothing for you, but DEATH.**"

Many traitors of the Moorish Nation have taken the position of presenting Noble Drew Ali from the perspective of a religious leader instead of a Constitutionalist. Misconceptions presented by those who should be in full support of teaching correct perspectives have created an atmosphere where even modern-European agent-provocateurs have a mockery mindset with regard to the teachings of Noble Drew Ali — and the Moorish Nation as a whole.

Noble Drew Ali was called by the great Universal Create-tress to save the nations from her wrath. In 2021, we are living in the midst of this wrath, witnessing daily the blatant disregard for *de jure* law, rights, spirituality, critical thinking etc, due to Noble Drew Ali's own people denying and neglecting his Prophethood. Instead, they chased after the Gods of Europe of whom they knew nothing.

"MOORISH SOVEREIGN CITIZENS"
Southern Poverty Law Centre.

> Further, according to Mark Pitcavage, a leading expert in the sovereign citizen movement, "Moorish sovereign citizens emerged in the mid-1990s on the East Coast when some people began to merge sovereign citizen ideas with some of the beliefs of the Moorish Science Temple, a religious sect dating back to 1913.

De facto agencies of the *de facto* U.S. corporation are not alone in this misinformation campaign being presented. They have also persuaded their little-sister corporation Canada to get involved in the fraudulent misrepresentation of the Moorish Nation.

"The History of the Organized Pseudolegal Commercial Argument Phenomenon in Canada," 2016
Canadian Legal Information Institute

> "Moorish Law" or "Moorish Nation" movement has emerged in black communities. While the Canadian OPCAsphere has surprising internal consistency, it is substantially different from the US Sovereign Citizen and Moorish Law variations. Each has its own conspiratorial and political focus, though all share the same ominous sense of impending tyranny and catastrophe."

When one studies Noble Drew Ali from sources other than those prepared by Drew Ali, it becomes clear that some individuals have purposefully sown misinformation about the Prophet Drew Ali. The subversion and confusion seeded within the Moorish Nation is not limited to specific organizations, it also influences perceptions within federal departments:

> FBI FILES: "HE STATED THAT HE IS NOT A NEGRO [BUT] BEY

HAS ALL THE **<u>APPEARANCE AND CHARACTERISTICS OF A NEGRO</u>**."

The FBI know who "Bey" is, yet imply Bey and Negro are the same. This is a deliberate attempt to cause confusion and slander Noble Drew Ali and ALL Moors. These slights serve as attempts to denationalize the Moors, putting them under wardship status, leaving them exposed to constant assumption of jurisdiction in issues of where citizenship diversity is the subject matter. It is easy for the FBI to stand in this fraudulent position when, as stated in *Aliities* by Spencer Dew, Grand Sheiks like Frederick Turner El told the FBI that Moors pledge allegiance to the United States.

Olajuwon Ali was known to police as a devotee of the Moorish Science Temple of America — it is interesting to note that Noble Drew Ali told the Moors not to use the name Ali. The FBI used Olajuwon to present Moorish Nationality as a black variation of the overwhelmingly "white" sovereign citizen movement; a domestic extremist ideology.

Olajuwon Ali Davis (left rear) at the Justice for Michael Brown Leadership Coalition in St. Louis. Nov. 2014.

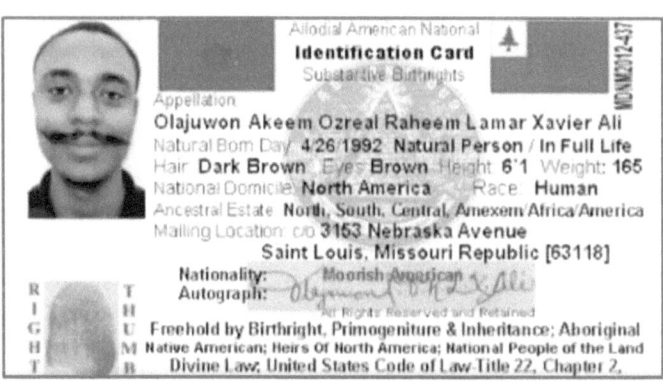

Moorish National Identification Card for Olajuwon Ali

"'Sovereign citizen' attacks a growing concern, police told"
Jim Bronskill, The Canadian Press
October 24, 2013

"A copy of the presentation was obtained by The Canadian Press under the Access to Information Act along with a pamphlet prepared by the chiefs of police that helps explain the Freeman-on-the-Land ideology. This movement is based on a decentralized, libertarian ideology, which is often motivated by personal gain, self-gratification or justification of illegal behaviour," says the pamphlet. The phenomenon has already attracted the attention of the Canadian Security Intelligence Service, which noted last year that law-enforcement agencies had seen "an increase in the number of incidents related to (Freeman) anti-government ideology in Canada." Other Canadian branches flagged by police in the briefing include the Moorish Divine and National Movement.

Rob Finch and Kory Flowers, Greensboro, N.C.

"A QUICK GUIDE TO SOVEREIGN CITIZENS"
UNC School of Government
Revised November 2013

Note: Much of the information for this paper was provided by detectives Rob Finch and Kory Flowers of the Greensboro, NC, Police Department, Amy Funderburk of the NC Administrative Office of the Courts, and David Adinolfi of the NC Attorney General's Office.

Names of their organizations

Two of the most prevalent sovereign citizens groups in North Carolina are the Moorish Nation and the Washitaw Nation. Moorish Nation adherents may refer also to the Moorish Science Temple, Moorish Republic, United Nuwaubian Nation of Moors (NUNM), MU'UR Republic or other variations. Moorish sovereigns tend to be black and younger; many get started on this path in prison. The Nation, a Moorish branch, is tied to a group in Poverty Point, Louisiana.

Buzzwords

Below are some unusual words or phrases or manner of punctuation or writing that are commonly used by sovereign citizens, reflecting their beliefs. Some of the words are legitimate legal terms in the proper context but are meaningless in the way they are used by sovereign citizens. For example, the Uniform Commercial Code (UCC) indeed exists and is important law for commercial transactions, but it has none of the purposes ascribed to it by sovereign citizens. It would take a long time to explain why sovereign citizens speak and write the way they do, or the meanings of these particular words; just be aware that the recurrence of these ways of communicating is one indicator that the person is a sovereign citizen.

Strawman	UN Indigenous People's Seat 215
Indigenous	Debtor is transmitting utility
De facto government	Use of "near" with zip code U.S.
Non-resident alien	Minor, Outlying Islands
Conveyance (rather than vehicle)	Special Trust Deposit In Admiralty
Traveling in a private capacity	Dishonor in commerce Accepted for value
References to UCC	
Use of red ink	Thumbprints on documents
IRS Form 1099-OID	Executor
Sui juris	Common law Final solution
Travelling in a commercial capacity	Man on the land Free man
Redemption	Referring to the government as a corporation
Aboriginal	
El Bey	Requesting an official's bond
Who is the victim?	Affidavit of truth
Where is your oath of office?	Fiduciary
© after a person's name	Judicial District of Tens Letters of Marque
Brackets around a zip code	
"Employer ID Number" rather than SSN	Title 4 flag Sovereign Living Soul UCC-1 Statement UCC-1-207
Domicile	Silence is acquiescence
Reference to HJR-192	Citizen
Charge Back Notice	

"Excerpt from Response To Finch and Flowers"
By Rahsmariah Bey, Publisher R.V. Bey Publications

Moors are by blood, jus sanguine, the true aboriginal people of the land, the American National, which by that mere fact they are in fact the ONLY sovereign. They are not "Black" sovereigns, nor is Noble Drew Ali a black separatist, and they are not a part of the Patriot Movement. More so over, neither the Patriot group or Moors are acting in an anti-government manner. It is the actions of **Finch** and **Flowers** and any other citizen who colludes with them that are in fact anti-government. To say that Moors are anti-government or that they are Black Sovereigns is a misrepresentation and by it being printed, is not only slanderous, it is libel. **Finch** and **Flowers** are descendants of naturalized citizens themselves and do not have any political rights or power here, except to follow the Law of the Land as Public Servants and Trustees. Their clear intent and organized mission to maintain violations of the people's rights is Treasonous. For that reason they ought to continue to be made responsible for their misrepresentation and abuse of their limited authority, if they have any at all. Otherwise they are on a personal mission and still they must be held accountable for their infractions and for breaking the law.

It is clear that they are attempting to muddy up the waters of "sovereignty" as to what it is and what it is not. Europeans could NEVER be sovereigns here. Sovereignty comes with nationality, it does NOT stand alone. Therefore, there is no validity to a so-called "Black Sovereign" or "Black Sovereignty Movement," nor is there validity to the Patriot groups who attempt to be sovereigns. The only sovereign here is the Moor American National. Of course then, a people of European descent would like for this to be their "homeland," void of sovereigns as they cannot be the sovereign and they don't want you to claim your nationality, thus your sovereign status. That is why they get upset when one proclaims their Nationality as that of a Moor. A Moor does NOT have to claim sovereignty, they have to declare their Nationality, and be themselves, the heirs apparent. Upon declaring their nationality and being themselves, sovereignty is bestowed. This puts a clear light on why those who have been usurping and violating the rights of the natural people, do not want to give up the ghost now, as they would then find themselves without food on their plate, without any bodies to rob liberties from. This is evident and translates as them being sued for *those violations of law.*

Their robbing of the people is why they have been prosperous and it is a commission of piracy.

Piracy*: A robbery or forceable depredation on the high seas, without lawful authority, done animo furandi in the spirit and intention of universal hostility. (Note: Animo means "with intent;" and furandi means "an intention of stealing").*

Under What Authority Do Finch and Flowers Act?:

*Their intentions, down to the "Intelligence Group" established by Private Detectives for the State of North Carolina - Detectives **Flowers** and **Finch**, are clear prima facie evidence of those who are and those who intend to collude as co-conspirators. As well, and even more important, they have published evidence of their committing of, but not limited to: **stalking, harassment, violation of privacy, unauthorized investigation, piracy, Fraud, Slander, Libel and acting as if they have Delegation of Authority, therefore impersonating an "Officer of the Court."** That is just for starters. All of these things are a violation of the Constitutionally secured rights of the people, of which they (Public Trustees / Public Officials / All Government Entities and their enclaves, are vowed by oath and affirmation to protect, preserve and secure. If they are acting on their own then they are **<u>renegades of the law and are but outlaws themselves</u>**. Any enforcement they make on the people are without authority and they ought be charged by the people for such violations, they ought not be surprised that they have been and will continue to be sued for violations of the peoples rights, thereby for bringing injury to the people. There exist NO Delegation of Authority that allows them to violate the Constitution and the People's Rights. They perform these acts under the guise of a government officer, which is in violation of **Title 18, Section 912 - Piracy**. They also perform these felonious acts under trickery and deceit, which falls under the definition of "Fraud". Please* *keep in mind that governments are only established for the purpose of protecting the rights of the people. Therefore all Public Trustees/ Officers / Magistrates / Judges / Agencies of any government / associations / corporations, et al **have an obligation** to speak and not be silent when they see or witness an infraction of the people's rights. Being silent constitutes Fraud!!!*

Without the marvelous light of knowledge of self brought by Noble Drew Ali, there would not be such a precise, competent response from Mother Rahs Bey. Without the jurisprudence teachings of the Noble Prophet Drew Ali, rvbeypublications.com may not even have existed for us today. One of the first challenges Noble Drew Ali overcame to establish our people's competency at law was to correct our status. While most individuals from most autochthonous/ aboriginal/ indigenous groups/ associations/ organizations today teach of status correction and how to go about it, i.e. processes and papers to file, they do so without acknowledging the FOUNDER of status correction: Noble Drew Ali. His teaching that we are not Negro, Black, Coloured or Ethiopian was not angry-Black-man ranting. This was done with the specific purpose of removing us from the dead status into a higher status where we can make/ file claims against those oppressing us. Many people look at the slave brands Negro, Black, and Coloured as identities when there are actuality basic terms used to introduce unconscious Moors into the realm of law.

101 Koran Questions for Moorish Children
88. What does coloured mean? Coloured means anything that is painted, stained, varnished or died.

Key words: ANY and THING. If you are a sentient, cognizant being you are for sure not a thing. Reading the definitions of *color* and *colored* in a law dictionary should inspire a greater respect for Noble Drew Ali, why he taught us that we are not colored, and why we should not identify as such.

Black's Law Dictionary
Fourth Edition with Pronunciation, 1957

COLOR. An appearance, semblance, or simulacrum, as distinguished from that which is real. A prima facie or apparent right. Hence, a deceptive appearance; a plausible, assumed exterior, concealing a lack of reality; a disguise or pretext.

COLORED. By common usage in America, this *term*, in such phrases as "colored persons," "the colored race," "colored men," and the like, is used to designate negroes or persons of the African race, including all persons of mixed blood descended from negro ancestry. But where a state Constitution provided for separate schools for the white and colored races, the term "white race" was held to be limited to the Caucasian race, and the term "colored races" to embrace all other races.

It has also been held that *there is no legal technical signification to the phrase "colored person" which the courts are bound judicially to know*.

"The Journey From 'Colored' To 'Minorities' To 'People Of Color'"
Kee Malesky
March 30, 2014

The *Act to Prohibit the Importation of Slaves into any Port or Place Within the Jurisdiction of the United States,* signed in 1807, which applied to "any negro, mulatto, or person of colour," indicates that the term was well-enough established to be used in the text of legislation. A 1797 survey of the population of what is now Haiti described three classes of people, including "The class which, by a strange abuse of language, is called people of colour, originates from an intermixture of the whites and the blacks."

In 1912, one year before Noble Drew Ali began teaching us to reject these fraudulent labels, the states of Kentucky, Maryland, Mississippi, North Carolina, Tennessee and Texas asserted that "a person of color" is one who is descended from a Negro to the third generation, inclusive, though one ancestor in each generation may have been white. According to the law of Alabama one is "a person of color" who has had any Negro blood in his ancestry for five generations. ... In Arkansas "persons of color" include all who have a visible and distinct admixture of African blood. Thus, it would seem that a **Negro in one state is not always a Negro in another**. That last line is proven in the William Dungey case where Abraham Lincoln stated "My client is not a Negro, though it is a crime to be a Negro–no crime to be born with a black skin. But my client is not a Negro. His skin may not be as white as ours, but I say he is not a Negro, though he may be a Moore." At that time Lincoln interrupted Judge Davis, saying, "You mean a Moor, not Moore." "Well, your Honor, Moor, not C.H. Moore," replied Lincoln. "I say my client may be a Moor, but he is not a Negro."

Salvador Vidal-Ortiz summed it up well in the Encyclopedia of Race, Ethnicity and Society:

"People of color explicitly suggests a social relationship among racial and ethnic minority groups. ... [It is] is a term most often used outside of traditional academic circles, often infused by activist frameworks, but it is slowly replacing terms such as racial and ethnic minorities. ... In the United States in particular, there is a trajectory to the term — from more derogatory terms such as negroes, to colored, to people of color. ... People of color is, however it is viewed, a political term, but it is also a term that allows for a more complex set of identity for the individual — a relational one that is in constant flux."

The psychological attack against the identity of the unconscious Moors continues with the new phrase BIPOC: Black Indigenous People of Color.

Remove "Indigenous," and you have the adjectives used to colonize the minds of the aboriginal Moors of America

> "We understand that under colonialism African and Indigenous people had very different experiences and to conflate everything in one is to erase, which is the very nature of genocidal practice." – Dr. Charmaine Nelson

Hadith and Prophesies of Noble Drew Ali

89. Bro. J. Blakely Bey said that the Holy Prophet told the Moors, "**Not throw away your slave names (your family last name), because we have a birth right under them. For the work that our ancestors did in slavery time, we will be paid off for this, and with compounded interest."**

239. Sis. Whitehead El stated that the Holy Prophet said "**Our nationality in this government began with the parade."**

Moorish Guide Newspaper, Feb. 1929

Divine Constitution and By Laws and MSTA/MHTS Charter

The Holy Prophet said, "A good Moorish leader must study his Holy Koran and Divine Constitution and By-laws."

What is a CONSTITUTION?

*In public law, the organic and fundamental law of a nation or state, which may be written or unwritten, establishing the character and conception of its government, laying the basic principles to which its internal life is to be conformed, organizing the government, and regulating, distributing, and limiting the functions of its different departments, and prescribing the extent and manner of the exercise of sovereign powers. In a more general sense, any fundamental or important law or edict...(*Black Law Dictionary 4th Ed.)

The drafting of a constitution by Noble Drew Ali is a sign to the Moors that we are a Nation, that we have a government, and we have sovereign power. According to Moorish literature, Noble Drew Ali stated that, "I brought you everything it takes to save a nation take it and save yourself." He also said, "This is not **no social organization** it is a Divine and National Movement. By you being born here don't make you a citizen. Look what I have on, now this was handed to me by the government. It represents the Royal Prince."

Hadith and Prophesies of Noble Drew Ali

220. Bro. J. Blakely Bey said that the Holy Prophet Noble Drew Ali said "**that the Grand Sheik of a Temple should go to the Temple, hang the Charter on the wall, say the Moorish American prayer, when it is time for the meeting to open, and if no one comes to the meeting after he sits and waits for one and half hours, then take the Charter down off the wall and go home.**"

What is a CHARTER?

An instrument emanating from the sovereign power, in the nature of a grant, either to the whole nation, or to a class or portion of the people, or to a colony or dependency, and assuring to them certain rights, liberties, or powers. (Black Law Dictionary 4th Ed.)

Group photo at the First National Convention of the MST of A. Chicago, 1928

Holy Koran MSTA / MHTS: The End of Time and the Fulfilling of the Prophesies

4. The Moorish Science Temple of America is a lawfully chartered and incorporated organization. Any subordinate Temple that desires to receive a charter; the Prophet has them to issue to every state throughout the United States, etc.

Noble Drew Ali surrounded by Chicago's top politicians. Chicago, 1928

Group photo of the First National Convention of the MST of A, Unity Hall. Chicago, 1928

When we connect everything — these institutions, instruments and literature presented to the Moors by Noble Drew Ali — we see that each has a unique function in guiding our placement in the affairs of men a.k.a. governing ourselves as all other nations do. The Charter, through the Divine Constitution placed in the Moorish Science Temple/Moorish Holy Temple of Science, assures the Moorish Americans of certain rights, liberties, and powers that come only through the proclamation of Moorish Nationality. This is outlined in Act 1 and Act 6 of the Divine Constitution and By Laws wherein:

Act 1. The Grand Sheik and the chairman of the Moorish Science Temple of America is in power to make law and enforce laws with the assistance of the Prophet and the Grand Body of the Moorish Science Temple of America. The assistant Grand Sheik is to assist the Grand Sheik in all affairs if he lives according to Love, Truth, Peace, Freedom, and Justice and it is known before the members of the Moorish Science Temple of America.

Act 6. — With us all members must proclaim their nationality and we are teaching our people their nationality and their divine creed that they may know that they are a part and a parcel of this said government, and know that they are not Negroes, Colored Folks, Black People, or Ethiopians, because these names were given to slaves by slave holders in 1779 and lasted until 1865 during the time of slavery, but this is a new era of time now, and all men now must proclaim their free national name to be recognized by the government in which they live and the nations of the earth, this is the reason why Allah the great God of the universe ordained Noble Drew Ali, the Prophet to redeem his people from their sinful ways. The Moorish Americans are the descendants of the ancient Moabites who inhabited the North Western and South Western shores of Africa.

Issuing Nationality and Identification cards

Hadith and Prophesies of Noble Drew Ali
242. Bro. J. Blakely Bey stated that the Holy Prophet said "**Moors, it will take you ten years to know what is on your nationality card, and you will be eighteen years in understanding what I have come for and what I have done.**"

In 2008, the Moorish Science Temple of America Temple #5 in Canaanland was established under the guidance of Brothers Heru Ranesi El, Mentu Bey, Aki Bey, Dawiyd Ali El and Kenu Bey. In 2021 we are still only scratching the surface of what Noble Drew Ali prepared and its application for the Moors in Canaanland. We have seen many join the temple just to get their Nationality Card and leave without showing any honour, respect, allegiance or making any sacrifice for Noble Drew Ali and the Moorish Divine and National Movement. Noble Drew Ali issued Nationality Cards because indigenous peoples and individuals are free and equal to all other peoples, and individuals and have the right to be free from any kind of discrimination in the exercise of their rights, in particular that based on their indigenous origin or identity. The right to personal identity is recognized in international law through a range of declarations and conventions. Theodore McCombs teaches that The twentieth century has witnessed horrific assaults on personal and group identity, including forced disappearances, child trafficking through illegal adoptions, and forced assimilation. These three classic identity rights violations highlight the importance of identity interests and provide context for the right to identity's ultimate codification in the Convention on the Rights of the Child. When we look through international documents addressing the rights of children, human beings and indigenous peoples, all of them state the right to a nationality. Considering all these international documents were issued after Noble Drew Ali, it is clear that the international community recognized, without acknowledgment, the lessons of nationality from Prophet Noble Drew Ali. When you research the leaders of so called black people, the only individual that told our people to get rid of slave brands and proclaim their nationality was Noble Drew Ali. Even if the Constitution does not expressly include a "right to identity," one may deduce such a right from its principles and positively recognized rights. The Convention on the Rights of the Child (CRC) explicitly protects the child's right to identity.

Article 8(1) provides:

States parties undertake to respect the right of the child to preserve his or her identity, including nationality, name, and family relations as recognized by law without unlawful interference.

Patrick McCarthy argues, on the basis of the CRC that "identity" is limited to nationality, name, and identity. Hence the importance of viewing everything Noble Drew Ali brought from an international law perspective. This is why the Holy Prophet told the Moors, "I brought you your nationality, your religion, and title to your vast estate. What do you want me to do; kill you?" The title to your vast estate is your El, Al, Bey, Dey and Ali that makes you Moorish by pedigree and descent. Our Nationality is Moorish American and is qualified in the *101 Questions* when he told us why we are Moorish American: because we are descendants of Moroccans BORN in America. *Nationality is defined as "that quality or character which arises from the fact of a person's belonging to a nation or state."* (http://hrlibrary.umn.edu/edumat/studyguides/noncitizens.html). *Nationality determines the political status of the individual, especially with reference to allegiance; while domicile determines his civil status. Nationality arises either by birth or by naturalization. According to Savigny, "nationality" is also used as opposed to "territoriality," for the purpose of distinguishing the case of a nation having no national territory; e. g., the Jews.* (Blacks Law Dictionary, 4th Ed.)

If Noble Drew Ali said you are born Moorish American but Moors under Temple #13 in Baltimore teach one must naturalize to be Moorish American, does it take a university degree to see the blatant contraction?

Hadith and Prophesies of Noble Drew Ali

101. Bro. T. Booker-Bey. G.N.T. (Emeritus) said that he was walking down the street in Chicago, Illinois, and an Arabian came out of a store, and asked him to come into the store. He went with him. The Arabian pointed at a man, and asked him. "Do you know who this is?" Bro. Booker-Bey said, "That is my Prophet." The Holy Prophet said, "**all right son**". The store was full of Arabians, and Bro. T. Booker-Bey said that all of them had Nationality Cards for the Moorish Science Temple of America.

Self-determination means that the individual is ultimately responsible for deciding and fashioning their own identity, no matter how much influence family, society, and the state may exert on them. The principle of self-determination necessarily indicates that an individual's identity is "pre-legal," in that it exists "independent of any positive juridical recognition." Dynamism refers to the continuous evolution of an individual's identity, thus, an individual may change his religion, or his family, or his name. *Professor Ya'ir Ronen describes this dichotomy as "the need to become" and "need to be." The first need refers to the individual's development and the constant recreation of her identity as she pursues her ambitions. The second need emphasizes the principle of authenticity, the individual's need to be true to her own self, at whatever stage in her development she finds herself, and the need for society to recognize this persona.* ((Right to Identity International Human Rights Law Clinic, University of California, Berkely, Nov. 2007). Again we see the master mind of Noble Drew Ali teaching the Moors to Be Themselves, as this in law means to be *in propria persona*. If pleaded or re-presented by an attorney, you are not being yourself and admit the jurisdiction.

This goes back to why we are not Negro, Black or Coloured. Accepting those labels mean we are not being ourselves. *Yvonne Donders suggests that the right to cultural identity has no abstract content. Rather than protect a general right to cultural identity, she proposes developing the "cultural dimensions" of the rights that protect language, property, and other specific aspects of cultural identity.* (Ibid 12).

Several international law scholars have attempted to define the right to identity through a relational lens, either as an overarching right that captures constitutive rights, or as a core right that conceptually unifies a series of related rights. Regardless of which way the pendulum swings, Noble Drew Ali issuing national identification cards was way before its time. Many opportunists have come into the Moorish movement with a fleece-the-people-approach to identity cards. They attempt to reinvent the wheel, adding spokes upon spokes upon spokes to an already well established form of identification created by C.M. Bey's Great Seal National Association of Moorish Affairs. These cards include picture, height, weight, hair and eye colour, codified laws, *stare decisis* and mailing location. Noble Drew Ali told the Moors Your nationality card is going to change in your pocket.

National Identification Card for the Moorish Science Temple of America

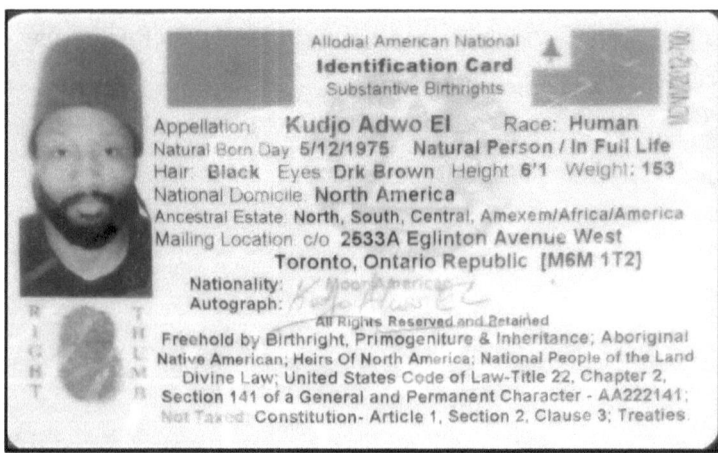

Moorish National Identification Card for Grand Sheik Kudjo Adwo El

Moorish Flag

101 Koran Questions for Moorish Children

19. What kind of a flag is the Moorish? It is a red flag with a five pointed green star in the center.

20. What do the five points represent? Love, Truth, Peace, Freedom and Justice.

21. How old is our flag? It is over 50,000 years old.

Flags are important to countries not only because they describe the authority and power of the nation, but because it is a symbol of peace and unity among the people allying themselves under that flag. Noble Drew Ali taught that this is the UNITING of Asia and that one of the points in the flag represents "peace." People who have doubts as to whether Noble Drew Ali is a Prophet must look at these actions he took and lessons he taught. No leaders of our people ever mentions a National flag in their presentations, most of them giving the people a banner instead. While flags and banners certainly bear a superficial resemblance, there is an important difference between the two. *The practice of flying flags indicating the country of origin outside of the context of warfare became common with the maritime flag, introduced during the age of sail, in the early 17th century.* (Wikipedia.org/flags).

Anything to do with Maritime is connected to the Moors. The Moors were the original seafarers and even the history of piracy on the seas has its origin with the Moors. In the Early Middle Ages, during the westward expansion of Islamic armies across Africa, traditions concerning flags were established that continue to influence flag use today. When the ruling dynasties of Morocco, the "Farthest West," acted independent of control from Cairo or Istanbul, their flags were characterized by a single colour (usually red or white), with or without inscriptions. Morocco being the farthest west is part of the reason Noble Drew Ali re-established the Moroccan flag opposed to any other for the Moors in America, and in turn the World. The red flag with the green five-point star is not just national, but empirical; Noble Drew Ali connected us to the Moroccan flag not for the Kingdom of Morocco but the Moroccan Empire.

About the Geometry of a Five-Point Star
By Jennifer Uhl
Sciencing.com
March 13, 2018

A five pointed star is a common symbol on flags and in religion. A golden five pointed star, is a star that has points of equal length and equal angles of 36 degrees at each point.

Function

A five pointed star is a common ideogram in many concepts throughout the world, and is featured on many flags and in religious symbols as well.

Features

When a five pointed star is drawn using points of equal length along with 36 degree angles at each point, then the five pointed star is often referred to as a golden five pointed star. The pentagram is the simplest regular star polygon, containing ten points. Five points make up the tips of the star, and five points make up the vertices of the inner pentagon.

The pentagram or five point star also consists of fifteen different line segments. By joining the collinear edges of the five point star together, a pentagon is produced. Like a regular pentagon, and like a regular pentagon that has a pentagram constructed within it, the regular pentagram has the dihedral group of order 10 as its symmetry group.

Considerations

Not only does a standard five point star have a pentagon in its middle, but when you connect the five points together with line segments, you will have created a proportional pentagon on its outer edges as well. Additionally, you can form a golden five point star using a series of embedded pentagrams.

Size

While not all five pointed stars have to possess points of the same length and points of equal angles, golden five pointed stars are perfect in this regard. A regular polygon, like the one that sits in the center of a five pointed star, has equal angles of 108 degrees each. The points of a golden five pointed star are all 36 degrees each, making the other two angles of each point of the star 72 degrees each. Five pointed stars can have points with unique line segment lengths and different angled points, but these are not golden five pointed stars, meaning that their points are not equal to one another.

Identification

The only characteristic that makes a five pointed star what it is, is possessing five points constructed from connecting line segments. The rules relating to golden five pointed stars are much more specific, however, dictating specific angles and equal lengths of each of the five points.

6. The Moabites from the land of Moab who received permission from the Pharaohs of Egypt to settle and inhabit North-West Africa; they were the founders and are the true possessors of the present Moroccan Empire. With their Canaanite, Hittite, and Amorite brethren who sojourned from the land of Canaan seeking new homes.

7. Their dominion and inhabitation extended from North-East and South-West Africa, across great Atlantis even unto the present North, South, and Central America and also Mexico and the Atlantis Islands; before the great earthquake, which caused the great Atlantic Ocean.

How a Pandemic Ended a Moroccan Empire
Ronan O'Connell
December 10, 2020

NOTE: *An invisible assassin snuck into Chellah and Rabat in the mid-1300s and decimated this area. The Black Death had arrived. Morocco had been afforded time to prepare its response to this bubonic plague pandemic. This infectious disease, which ended up killing more than 25 million people worldwide in just five years, had been rampant in Europe for many months before it leaped the Strait of Gibraltar and crashed into Morocco. The eerie way the Black Death emerged and its horrifying effects on the human body make COVID-19 pale by comparison. It exploded across Europe due to a squadron of so-called "death ships." In October of 1347, the southern Italian seaside city of Messina welcomed 12 vessels from Central Asia. Italian port workers boarded these ships to find a scene seemingly transplanted from a nightmare. Each boat was littered with disease-ridden corpses. The surviving sailors resembled zombies, their malnourished bodies laden with enormous, bloody boils.*

As the saying goes: history repeats itself.

The law of the flag doctrine provides that a merchant ship is part of the territory of the country whose flag she flies. Visualize the Moorish Divine and National Movement as the ship. Actions aboard that ship are subject to the laws of the flag state. The laws of the flag state are the Divine Constitution and By-Laws along with any rules and customs adopted or enforced by Moorish leadership. Jurisdiction may be exercised concurrently by a flag state and a territorial state. This last fact is why Jurisdiction is always challenged by Moors due to the diversity of citizenship based on our flag. Colonial officers and agents having no *personum*, subject matter nor territorial jurisdiction in any affairs involving Moors. While Noble Drew Ali bringing our flag may not immediately trump a *de facto* sovereign's territorial jurisdiction to prosecute violations of its "laws," it absolutely demolishes it once Status is brought up as the first issue during adjudication.

Colour of law applies to colourable people, which again is why Noble Drew Ali said we Moor are not coloured, so colourable law is not to be assumed nor applied. Our Moroccan flag establishes our Status and Jurisdiction and proves diversity if the oppressors are flying their banner. Banners are not National flags and do not excuse colourable activity. Sheikess Nika El Bey taught that once the people fall under a banner instead of a flag, then those people are under a national ban. *Ban* is Old English *bannan:* "to summon, command, proclaim," from Proto-Germanic **bannan* "to speak publicly" (used in reference to various sorts of proclamations), "command; summon; outlaw, forbid". Our people claiming a banner are actually outlawed and are classified as Ruthless.

If you are Ruthless you are stateless and have no ancestral honour. Moors are descendants of the Ancient Moabites and to deny your nationality is to deny your National flag and your Ancient foremothers and forefathers. The National flag Act of Canada states, *Whereas the Canadian flag is the symbol of the nation's unity; Whereas the Canadian flag represents the principles of freedom, democracy, courage, and justice upon which our great nation is based;*

Does that sound familiar?

101 Koran Questions for Moorish Children

30. What was the nationality of Ruth? Ruth was a Moabitess.

31. What is the modern name for the Moabites? Moroccans.

32. Where is the Moroccan Empire? Northwest Amexem.

33. What is the modern name for Amexem? Africa.

Parts of Africa are found under America, and in America there are place names like Algiers, Louisiana; Cairo, Illinois; Cairo, Ohio; Karnak, Illinois; Luxor, Pennsylvania; Memphis, Tennessee — clearly America is also Africa/Amexem.

National Headdress

Hadith and Prophesies of Noble Drew Ali

244. Bro. J. Blakely Bey stated that the Holy Prophet said "**dont think that a fez or a turban on your head makes you a Moslem, Moslems are born, not made.**"

Little is conclusively known of the turban's origin. The earliest evidence of a turban-like garment is from a royal Mesopotamian sculpture dating circa 2350 B.C.E. As the turban was in use before the advent of Judaism, Islam and Christianity, the origin of the turban cannot be ascribed to religious reasons alone. Though being the founders of religions, our ancestors did not have a religious mindset.

Turbans were originally worn by royalty and spiritual leaders and were used to commute power, often being decked out with jewels and accessories to display the wealth and grandeur of the wearer or the culture they belonged to. Naysayers constantly call Noble Drew Ali religious, but the headwear he brought for the Moors was in use *before* Islam, so it is no wonder the Prophet told Moors to return to the state of mind of our ancient foremothers and forefathers. The Moorish styled turban as a headdress for Moorish Americans is not merely a fashion statement or cultural paraphernalia; it has spiritual, metaphysical symbolic meaning beyond the obvious as a headwear. It serves to identify and distinguish the wearer as a member of the Moorish Nation, is diverse in nationality, and is **not** Negro, Black, Coloured or Ethiopian. Insulting the turban was an intolerable offence to one's personality—in the Bible, the Prophet Isaiah states, "When God takes away the turban, he takes away the dignity of man."

Detail of an entrance gate to the Chandra Mahal at the City Palace Jaipur, Rajasthan, India

Thousands of years ago, yogis and spiritual seekers discovered that the hair on the top of the head protects the "soft spot" from sun and exposure. Asiatic hair acts as antennae, channeling the energy and life-force of the sun into the body and brain. To amplify the effect, spiritual seekers would coil or knot their hair at the tenth gate (soft spot) – also called the solar center of the head. In men, the solar center is on top of the head at the front (anterior fontanel). It is important to note that women have two solar centers: one is at the center of the crown chakra, the other is on top of the head towards the back (posterior fontanel). For men and women, coiling or knotting the hair at the solar centers focuses the energy and helps retain a spiritual vibration throughout the day.

Turbans cover the temples, which is said to help protect a person from the mental or psychic negativity of other people and their environment. The pressure of the turban also changes the pattern of blood flow to the brain. Noble Drew Ali brought us the turban so we can crown ourselves as people of Universal Consciousness who sit on the throne of commitment to our own higher Self realization and activation. Wrapping the turban is a spiritual practice like wrapping a mummy or wrapping copper around crystals, where we take the highest, most visible part of ourselves – our head – and show that it belongs to the Creator. Wearing the turban also helps cultivate a sense of surrender to the Divine because, depending on the length of the cloth used, this can turn into a very intense meditation. The turban becomes a flag of the Moorish American consciousness as well as a crown of spiritual esoteric divine royalty.

Noble Prophet, Drew Ali

The feather symbolizes truth; that which must rise, also of lightness, dryness, the heavens, height, speed, spaciousness, and flight to the other realm. The expression "a feather in your cap" is used to mean honor to you; it refers to the custom among many cultures of adding a feather in the hat after an achievement. Ostrich feathers mean distinction. A feathered helmet is a triumph. Wearing feathers helps the Moor take on the powers of the birds, including transcendence, instinctual knowledge, and flight. Feathers are omens of light burdens and even of attainment of goals.

The Moorish Turban
A.C. / M.S.T.A. 24

The Turban is not only worn as a casual headdress, it is also worn as a HOLY CROWN, as evidenced by the PROPHET in his most ancient royal garb. The headdress is worn universally by Moslems throughout the Asiatic Nations of the Earth Land.

Bust of a Proud Oriental. cir. 1900

THE TURBAN represents the CIRCLE of which is 360 degrees. Just as the Moorish Fez, this wrapping or crowing of the head is the sealing of the forehead by the Head, Chief Angel.

Most times the Turban is wrapped right over left and when done this way, it represents higher self over lower self, right over wrong, etc. When wrapped left over right it represents the seen and the unseen; with the left side (seen) representing the flesh, and the right side in this case represents the unseen spirits of ALLAH. The Moorish American of today prefer the mentioned (right over left).

The colors of the Moorish Turban are very significant as the Prophet said that we Moors could wear the colors of the rainbow. Therefore, the representations of the colors come in, with the basic colors being RED, GREEN, and BLUE. The RED as we know represents DIVINE LOVE/ BLOOD; GREEN represents NOURISHMENT/ EARTH and FERTILITY; BLUE represents ROYALTY. GOLD represents the HEALING POWERS of EARTH; PURPLE represents THE RULER, and WHITE, of course, represents PURITY; BLACK represents DEATH and worn by the adept as they are those who have attained unto a measure of faith; the adept has gained enough faith to be firmly rooted in Drew Ali, thus escaping death of which is the state that the Prophet found us. Colors such as BROWN, BEIGE, TAN, etc., are tones of THE EARTH LAND in tune with NATURE. The color YELLOW represents EXTREME CAUTION and is sometimes used to represent COWARDICE.

The Moorish turban is wrapped with a strip or two; the strip of cloth represents THE CORD that stretches from THE HEART OF MAN to the HEART OF ALLAH. This is the reason why we don't let the cords hang past our chest area, down to the area of the private parts; as we don't want to draw energy from these parts of the body, but only from the height of our frames. A woman is not restricted to, but usually wraps the turban with strips (cords) around her shoulders.

...the turban represents wisdom—the wisdom that speaks from the highest planes of spirit life. We know that this is the Motherly or feminine aspect of ALLAH. Woman is part of life or creation, and represents the WISDOM OF ALLAH; THE STILL SMALL VOICE, HOLY BREATH, ETC.

Lib at Large: Documentary tells odd story of Korla Pandit, 'godfather of exotica'
Paul Liberatore
October 29, 2015

R.J. Smith exposed the true identity in a 2001 article in Los Angeles Magazine, "The Many Faces of Korla Pandit." His fans were shocked to learn that their swami dream boat wasn't born in New Delhi, far from it. He wasn't even Indian. He was a light-skinned African American, born in Columbia, Missouri, in a family of seven children. His father was pastor of the largest black church in town and his mother was of Creole heritage. His real name was John Roland Redd. He attended a

John Redd, aka Korla Pandit

segregated school in Missouri and showed talent as a pianist and later as an organist.

Tracing Pandit's chameleon-like career, first as Juan Rolando, a persona he adopted in Southern California during a Latin music craze in the 1940s. By passing as Mexican, he was allowed to join the whites-only local branch of the Musicians Union. After California's law against mixed-race marriages was struck down in 1948, Pandit married a white woman, Beryl DeBeeson, an animator for Disney. By most accounts, she was instrumental in Rolando morphing into the inscrutable Hindu organ guru Korla Pandit. He's credited with probably being the first African American to have his own television show, even though he did it as an Indian. As Dr. Harry Edwards points out in the film, he did it for economic reasons because of the Jim Crow laws. Lassie could get a show on TV but Nat King Cole couldn't. Born at a time when a black man in the South could get whipped for making eye contact with a white woman, Korla Pandit was making dreamy eyes at thousands upon thousands of aproned homemakers, stealing into their dens as they heated their fondue pots. In piecing together the puzzle of Pandit's life, the filmmakers interviewed a number of celebrities, including Carlos Santana, who had watched Pandit's show as a kid growing up in Tijuana. In his typical helium-filled manner of speaking, Santana says Pandit was "beyond time and gravity."

The fez used to be common headwear in Mediterranean countries and originated from Morocco, the Land of the Moors. After the fall of the Moors it was a popular among Ottoman elites, until it was banned in Turkey.

The Intriguing History of the Fez Hat You'd Love to Read Through MenWit.com

When the Hajj pilgrimage was temporarily suspended in 980 AD, pilgrims living to the western side of the Nile river were directed to Fez as an alternative to the Holy City of Mecca. In Fez, a Moor merchant started the supplies of a new style of headdress, which quickly became popular due to the heavy influx of pilgrims in the city. Fez initially had a monopoly on the manufacture of fezzes, because the berry used to color the hats was planted only there.

The fez again came up against a wall in 1925, when the new leader of Turkey, Kemal Ataturk, felt that it was a sign of being backward. He felt that traditional garments should be replaced by British suits and styles. To push Turkey towards alleged modernization, the fez was banned. However, this ban was not taken well by the people of the country, leading to several riots, and large numbers of fezzes being confiscated as illegal contraband. When an attempt was made to overthrow Ataturk, and bring back the fez, 9 – 10 people were shot and killed, virtually making the fez disappear.

Fez: A time-honored Ottoman hat from the Mediterranean
By Ekrem Bugra Ekinci
May 16, 2016

...Algerian men wore red fezzes. Poems were written about the fez, saying that it made a man more handsome. A song by Ottoman artist Rıfat Bey "Pek Yakıştı Eğri Fes" (A Crooked Fez Fits You Nicely) was very popular.

Adopted in 1925, an unprecedented law ordered men to wear

brimmed hats. Penalties were imposed on those who opposed this law. Wearing a fez was considered a crime.

How is that for denying a birthright? However, the tradition of wearing a fez was maintained in other countries like Syria, Iraq, Palestine, Egypt, Western Thrace, Macedonia and Bosnia, all countries which used to be part of the Ottoman Empire, which was originally the Moorish Empire. The fez never lost popularity in Tunisia, Libya, Morocco and Algeria. Remember: every time Moors wear their fez it is a symbol of national pride. The traditional red headwear is our sign of heightened intelligence, manhood and distinction. By wearing a fez, the wearer claims that they belonged to a highly evolved bloodline. The red fez symbolizes the "supreme height of practical wisdom".

Janelle Monaé, American Artist

Cam Newton, American Athlete

André 3000, American Artist   *Daffy Duck, Warner Bros. Cartoon*

The sombrero has utilitarian origins and Mexico's signature wide-brimmed hat was designed to protect wearers from the sun, taking its name from the Moorish Latin word for "shadow" or "shade." A sombrero can be any brimmed hat to Spanish speakers, but the word typically conjures images of Cinco de Mayo celebrants and mariachi bands. One popular theory of its origin traces it back to the Mestizo cowboys of Central Mexico — it has historically been linked to socioeconomic status.

Noble Prophet Drew Ali at Pan-American Conference Havana Cuba 1929

The Divine Origin of the Asiatic Nations

5. The Asiatic nations of North, South, and Central America: the Moorish Americans and Mexicans of North America, Brazilians, Argentinians and Chilians in South America.

6. Columbians, Nicaraguans, and the natives of San Salvador in Central America, etc. All of these are Moslems.

Feathered headdress, Aztec, reproduction
National Anthropology Museum, Mexico City

Cayuse women and girl in traditional headwear and garb, circa 1910

Hadith and Prophesies of Noble Drew Ali

179. Before the bank crash in 1929, Sister A. Brown El of Temple 4 and 25 said that the Holy Prophet told the Moors, "**if they had money in the bank, to get it out.**" Some said that the Prophet told the Moors to put their money in the post office. Those that obeyed the Holy Prophet saved their money, and those that did not, lost their money. Bro. C. Carriton Bey (past) G.G. of New York said that one day he was at the annual national convention, and Bro. C. Kirkman Bey sent for him to come outside to witness something. There was a European man, his wife, and daughter there. The European man asked Bro. C. Kirkman-Bey "Where is that little man that use to be around." Bro. C. Kirkman-Bey let them know that he was no longer with us. These Europeans started crying. They were looking for the Holy Prophet. That man was able to save his money during the bank crash, because he obeyed the Holy Prophet, and took his money out of the bank.

Honours to the Prophet Noble Drew Ali for bringing us EVERYTHING it takes to save a Nation and Honours to all Moors worldwide.

Other Titles By Kudjo El

Noble Drew Ali Plenipotentiaries

"Watch My Prophesies."

Well, Come to Klanada: Colour of Law & Authority on Usurped, Annexed, Moorish Land

You Are NOT Negro, Black, Coloured, Morisco, Nor an African Slave

Who Stole the Fez, Moors or Shriners

Nationality: The Order of the Day: Divine Message and Warning, All Garveyites, Rastafarians, Black Nationalists & Pan-Africans

Find G.S. Kudjo Adwo El Online

Email: CanaanlandMoors@gmail.com

RVBeyPublications.com

CalifaMedia.com/Kudjo-El

WillofAllah.com

YouTube: youtube.com/user/SutTekhEL

ustream.tv/channel/mhtonlinekanaanta

www.ingramcontent.com/pod-product-compliance
Lightning Source LLC
Chambersburg PA
CBHW030159100526
44592CB00009B/361